IT HAS COME TO THIS

Poets of the
Great Mother Conference

Special thanks to Gus Brunsman for proofreading and generous feedback.

Back cover image "Crows 104" by Meggan Gould.

Designed and edited by Chris Jansen.

ISBN   978-0-615-26210-9

Introduction   5

Kelli Allen   *Egg Stone*   7

Coleman Barks   *The Splinter and the Riversticks*   8

Robert Bly   *The Mourning Dove's Call*   10
                         An Improvisation Around Im   10

Pierre Boivin   *Tabla Rasa*   11

Henry Braun   *Dearest Reader*   12

Beth Philips Brown   *How The Mountain Forgives*   13

Gus Brunsman   *Relation Ship*   15

George Burns   *Younger, I Was a Racing Car*   16

Priscilla Carr   *In Her Fashion*   17

Stuart Chappell   *Spring Rain*   18

Tom Devine   *Small Group, Day 5*   19

Kathryn Fazio   *Fire With Fire*   20

Peter Felsenthal   *May in Maine*   21

Patricia Fiske   *Mudpies*   22

boB Henning   *Another Sleep Shortened Night Invested in The Soul* 23

Tina Holt   *Developing Heard Immunity*   24

Chris Jansen   *After the Fire Dance*   25

Steve Jeffries   *Fear of Poetry*   27

Cynthia Johnson   *This Morning*   28

Sioban Lanigan   *For Robert*   29

Gary Lawless	*May We Be Blessed*	31
Jim Lenfestey	*Easter Morning, 2004*	32
Jen Lighty	*The Song of the Ground*	33
Glenna Luschei	*Deep Gap Haiku*	35
Norm Minnick	*Henry Braun*	36
Trey Moore	*Anchorage*	37
Tammy Nelson	*Fall in Love with Your Life*	38
Margaret Paul	*Crows*	40
Nils Peterson	*Poem for Frederick*	41
Michael Quam	*Table Top*	42
Fran Quinn	*It Has Come To This*	43
Katie Rauk	*On the Sandhill Crane Migration Route in November*	44
Joe Shakarchi	*Stuttering Boy*	45
Myra Shapiro	*Reflection, This Fall*	47
Carol Sheldon	*Reporting From a Night on Lake Damariscotta*	48
Thomas R. Smith	*Lake Stone*	49
Barbara Spring	*At Palisades Nuclear Power Plant*	50
Frank Steele	*August Ending*	51
Peggy Steele	*Pebbles*	52
Echo Trobridge	*In the Company of Great People*	53
Jim Watt	*Seven Haiku for Summer 2008*	54
Phil Woods	*Gratitude In Telluride*	55

A Little Introduction

There is something about a book isn't there? As a member in good standing of the Skeptic Friends Network I'm not supposed to believe in magic, unquantifiable energies, or Akashic heavens. I don't. Yet there is something I can't explain that goes into a book. I know a woman who puts so much of herself into her books that just touching them will burn my fingers. Touching this book I feel the living energies of the conference-body. From the benevolent stones that Thomas Smith and Kelli Allen have gathered for us, to the great heart of Gus Brunsman and the wily energy of Pierre Boivin. I feel the blessings called down from heaven by Gary Lawless and Stuart Chappel, and the blessings rising up from the earth where Bob Henning and Glenna Luschei and Katie Rauk have been. There is the quiet, persistent wisdom of Jim Lenfestey and Jim Watt, and the urgency of Joe Shakarchi. And then there is love. So much love. The love that moves Norm Minnick and Tom Devine and Tina Holt and so many others. Most of all there is love. Can anyone read Nils Peterson or Fran Quinn without bringing their full heart? Can anyone read Henry Braun or Robert Bly or Coleman Barks without bringing their greatest soul? These poems do what all great poems do—they challenge us to match their largeness of feeling, to be more intuitive, to listen, to love, to be a little more than we were, even if that being-more manifests as being most contentedly ourselves.

Myself, I came late to this party. It was sometime around 1998 when an intuitive friend—a sorceress maybe—told me there was a conference put on every year by Robert Bly and that I needed to go. Soon. Unfortunately I was doing just fine back then. Didn't need anyone else. I had it all under control. A few years later things went to pieces in the way they so often do, and I found myself sitting in the grief house with a mouth full of ashes. I began to follow the path that Joseph Campbell says "seems to have been before you all the time," and it took me to, among other places, a lush green hillside in Wisconsin where people joined hands and sang, "In beauty, it's begun." How could anyone not fall in love with that?

When I asked for submissions for this anthology I wasn't sure what I'd get but I knew it would be good. My original idea was to collect and preserve poems from readers at the open mic poetry salons that are a regular part of the conference's afternoon schedule, so impressed was I by the incredible talents there. Some people asked for guidelines but I couldn't come up with any. "Just send what you feel is right," I said, trusting the reservoir of magic that brings poems into being and sends them where they need to go.

I said I don't believe in other worlds, yet here we are, our love energies admixed in such a way that there must be a wedding in some heaven. Now we go on, as Fran Quinn puts it, "until the gods of distance / fall asleep side by side / and dream us together again."

Chris Jansen
Athens, Georgia.

Egg Stone

How do we teach a stone thing
smoothness? We cannot know so much
about perfection. What are Saturn's rings
if not the curved rooms of the womb.

A mother's seed needs
to be translucent, but it does not
always understand the way to clarity.

The universe hatches in the same way
    over and over
and the human egg
is simply the lying stone.

We wrap our twenty white tongues
around the body of our mother before
we are even born.

Kelli Allen

The Splinter and the Riversticks

I get a splinter on the outside right
of my heel. I need help. I call Benjamin.
He says Come on over. I take a papersack
of implements: needle, tweezers, mirror, flashlight.
Tuck is hiding in the middle of the floor
under a thrown-off pile of blankets.
Are you ready to help?

I prop my leg high on a chairback.
Surgeon Benjamin. It's in sideways.
Tuck close in over his shoulder
like a second head holding the flashlight.
It's like finding a feather of hay
in a needlestack. You are too clever
for your own good, Tuck. I think I've got
part of it. These tweezers are so rusty.
They were in the back of the medicine cabinet.
Last time they were used was on my foot
forty years ago. This is blood poisoning central.
Rilke died from a thorn prick. Poets ought
to die from roses. A noble death.

I'll tell you a noble death.
I went to Sunny Pressly's funeral.
Big overflow crowd. The preacher said
Sunny didn't come to church much
but in hot summer he would quietly
back his pickup to the church steps
during the service and put big slices
of watermelon there, so that when
they came out from church they'd each have
a big cold sweet piece of watermelon.
Is that not true communion?
He would string them out down
the dinner-on-the-grounds counter too.
Kids loved him to pieces.

Let's leave the remnant in,
not good to dig too deep. Remember Achilles?
His one vulnerability was where his mother held him
when she dipped him in the River Styx.
She forgot she needed to douse him twice
to get the job done, holding him by the other heel.
So he had that one place where he could be hurt,
or killed, like me. My mother held me by the throat.
That's why I stammered, like Billy Budd.
I still have episodes of rage and jealousy
and disengaged passive aggression.
Otherwise, I am perfect and impervious.

Superman has kryptonite. Right.
That was so disturbing when Superman
went limp and flightless, a barely even
ordinary man. I know what riversticks are.
What? Ones that float by in a race. A logjam.
That was a riverstick I had in my foot.
If it were big enough, I could walk on water.
Or run. You could take off running. I'd be
strolling the side of a big moving hill
of ocean. Here comes the top of it
under me—now I'm on the other side.

Coleman Barks

9

The Mourning Dove's Call

The mourning dove's call woke me
In the still night, when it was still night
To me. Those sounds were older even
Than the box radio, and they said,
"Your mother is walking along the road.
I saw your dead father last night
Near the cottonwood grove."
I spent the night in a house with dear
Friends asleep in a neighboring room.
The call woke me in the still night.

(For Peggy and Frank)

Robert Bly

An Improvisation Around Im

The nimble ovenbird, the dignity of pears,
The simplicity of oars, the imperishable
Engines inside slim fir-seeds, all of these
Make clear how much we want the impermanent
To be permanent. We want the hermit wren
To keep her eggs even during the storm.
But that's impossible. We are perishable;
Friends, we are salty, impermanent kingdoms.

Robert Bly

10

Tabla Rasa

When the tabla begin to play
Your slate is wiped clean
And begins to be
Rewritten
All over again

Pierre Boivin

Dearest Reader

Alone, the girl Leisure
in the Book of Hours
(others all have places to go)
sits on her widest windowsill
gazing out on the now
hardly settled dust
of Tuesday, most pedestrian of days.
Moored in the image of my own
body simmering with feeling,
I'm there too
as voyeur on her side of the window,
invisible house guest
on my best
behavior.
"Helloooooooo!"
Before the sound of her voice I stand at attention.
Ah, let be!
Let both of us simply BE
to turn my pages quietly and read.

Henry Braun

How The Mountain Forgives

It doesn't argue or blame.

It doesn't even
care who's right or wrong
or who does things
the proper way.

It doesn't mind
if your feelings get hurt
or if the mistake
is large or small
of if you did your best.

It waits
in the way that mountains do.

Maybe tectonic plates shift.
Maybe lightning starts a fire.

Maybe no thing happens.
Maybe something invisible
smaller than an ant or cell wakes up.

The mountain waits,
letting the elements do
their work
and then it takes you in.

You wake up lichen,
pebble or bark,
maybe the fragrance of sage.

And then you realize
you can't remember
what the quarrel was about.

It's you and the mountain,
that sweetness like spring water

and always there like crisp air.

The mountain waits
in the way that mountains do.

Beth Philips Brown

Relation Ship

It's about eye to eye contact.
Soul to Soul contact.
Honoring one another.
Building a safe nest to contain the relationship...
Safe touch.
Interdependence instead of codependence
Pliable boundaries that expand and contract
Response instead of reaction...
Love...
    love of Self and others
Unconditional love ...

Gus Brunsman

Younger, I was a racing car

roaring towards the future.
Almost 6, almost 7, 10.

Was I ever 4, you asked.
Never. I was born 11.

Now, yesterday I just
wanted to stop
and look at your face.

But there wasn't time.

George Burns

In Her Fashion

It is not a major modulation.
Despair evolves into psychic
majority with the cadence
of blossoms disrobing a tree.
She disconnects the phone,
drops the Chevy on blocks
and holds the mail until spring.
Her habituated psyche hibernates
according to its chemistries and
        climactic rhythms.

Wolf Moon and Solstice
are her psychic markers.
Afraid of *her*, she complies
with internal mandates,
requiring a season without
human voice or touch.
Kitty offers his belly as a face mitten.
No betrayals by chocolate or alcohol;
only scientific diets for each and a
regimen of evening woodland walks
        and long afternoon siestas.

Phantom poets swear she sprouts
a tail and haunches,
while Pretty Kitty struts upright
and recites Dickinson.
They nestle in their insulated,
winter refuge made safe
for selves
and others.

Priscilla Carr

Spring Rain

The great storm
past banging,
flash and clapping
over lake and wood
leaving me wet.
Dripping raindrops
run down my face
mix with warm tears.
How happy I am
washed of life's
dust once again.

Stuart Chappell

Small Group, Day 5

For a moment:
   I forgot to paint their faces
   with the simple masks I make
   (this one's safety, that one's danger)
   so there's nothing more to seek...
In that moment, they became
themselves: enigmatic,
like magical lids on canopic jars,
  mysterious shapes of smile, squint, frown
     rippling their surfaces.
It was like waking up and knowing you're home.

Tom Devine

Fire With Fire

Fire with fire
a guitar in the mire,
In grasping for freedom
We cut the neck of a lute.
For the sake of one nation,
We decapitate whole societies.
In grasping for fruit we lean on the bowl,
And throw up the flute.
What the Witches of Eastwick
Could do with a cherry.

Kathryn Fazio

May in Maine

Surprised by peony
Suddenly tall out of earth
Finger size buds,
Pansy, white winter survivors,
Bloom wildly yellow, orange,
Few apple blossoms,
Cherry flaunt their glamour.
Across the river, soft pastel
Leaves slowly unfurl.

A cool dry spring

Lilac just beginning, forsythias finished
Air and light seriously call
Black flies ready for flesh
Early sunrise
Cream bearberry blooms fill with bees
Tulip colors the ground

Inhale flowers

Melt into breath

Peter Felsenthal

Mudpies

As a child, I put my parents in a pie
Encased them in muddy anger to dry
Kept them there til I was fully grown
Capable of decisions of my very own
Left them in mudpie, went my own way
Visited seldom for we had little to say
As the years passed, I grew and matured
But left them in mudpie, for I was inured
I didn't notice how they had grown too
Or care if they wanted to know me anew
They didn't grasp my growth, you see
When the mudpie melted, I found me

Patricia Fiske

Another Sleep Shortened Night Invested in The Soul

The stone is cool under my back
    this August morn.
It is the shadow
    of beech trees
        that heal me
           skin first.
All that is cold
    and dark
        is not awful.

boB Henning

Developing Heard Immunity

we were all there
listening to the woods, words, wards, warnings
woozy from the joy of hearing speaking truth.
hugs and sharing of all energies in forms of poetry and other life forms
the reaction to protect dropped, the sipping of others elixirs—
a virus we passed around—some became feverish and danced,
or fell to the ground in ecstasy;
or sat still and listened intently to the pulsations
some lost their voice and could only beam a scratchy hallelu by raised
eyebrows across the hall
the young kept running, playing, hardly slowing
the few stayed at a distance hoping to avoid full capture
circling, circling, the internal defenses of each rose to the occasion at
varying speeds
the moisture of dew beading on the brow
the internal furnace and production of protection
protecting, and placing the body firmly in the presence of self-non-self
home, recovered with days of lucid dreaming sleep
where did the week go
this congestion is now bursting forth, the protection from that
form of isolation settled into the blood stream
and the next time memory fades, and I share a toast, a hug, and poem
a song, I will be glad for the protection that being in this group gives,
having its heard immunity

Tina Holt

After the Fire Dance Was Over

my friend and I sat down
by the boathouse to talk.
What should we say now,
we who could find each other's wounds,
even in the dark if we wanted?
The dead gather a bouquet of silence,
as our eyes gather pinpricks of starlight,
as the lake gathers summer rain.
My friend says she can feel energy flowing
through the roots of enormous trees
and speak the language of stones,
touch the faces of the people trapped inside.
I don't hear anything from trees,
or stones, or even the stars that I love so much;
only the lake, whispering, *Careful, careful*
people have drowned in me.
After we die, these memories are
taken up into the world,
in the lake a few words, near the beach,
a rippling shadow,
long breaths of wind in the forest,
Tomorrow you too will walk in me.
So what is there left to say, dear friend?
We already recognize each other's face in the dark.
Tell me all my secrets.
I know who you are and I know why you've come.
Yes?
So we have an understanding then.
Yes.
I want you to tell me the story of your life
and I want to tell you mine.
Somewhere in the high darkness ghosts hold hands
and leap back into their bodies,
bodies hold hands and leap back into themselves...
I never told anyone this before
but since I was a kid I could kind of taste certain words.
It's not like you would think.
Love tastes bitter. *Sexy* is like salt.

Friendship is sort of peanut buttery
Fire tastes like licorice. *Death* is sweet.
Bullshit is sweeter than death,
sweeter even than ice cream,
which is also, coincidentally, very sweet.

Some of the lives among us last only one night,
but some nights last a lifetime:
I want you to tell me the story of your life
and I want to tell you mine.

Chris Jansen

Fear of Poetry

Some things are inside other things
but we have to stop and think.
The cold is couched in winter.
Flowers are within spring.
And poetry, if it's doing its job, sits in the lap of truth.
And truth…. has its beginnings and endings deep within the mythology
of the present.

It's the mythology that's so volatile.
Ever-so-slowly   shifting and moving.
A mist taken for granted with everyone shouting
"It's over here, it's over here!" Followed by a muffled—eyes shifting,
"I think."

Or perhaps we're in a temporary cauldron
boiling and stuffed to overflowing with transparent rituals.
Fed by a fiber optic fire hose,
popping with the sound of 9mm gunfire.

Or once upon a time, with a nearly unbearable sadness,
a three masted schooner sailed into Desolation Sound.
Raven took flight as 10,000 years of beginnings and endings
roared off the water.

I'm less afraid of poetry now.
But I know that uncomfortable feeling you have when I declare,
"Hey, I've just finished a new poem".

Steve Jeffries

This Morning

This morning
The sky is gray
Rain comes in sheets from
The southwest
The leaves gold red and bronze
Fly with the rain and
Land on the green glistening grass.

A small goat
An old goat
Down on her knees
Propped against a wall
Calls for her food.
Her water.

The veterinarian
Fills the syringe
With poison with her
Strong competent hands
While I hold the
Unsuspecting goat's head
Talk to her softly
Whisper sweet nothings
Until her eye clouds
And her head rests limp
        Against my arm.

Cynthia Johnson

For Robert

Listening
to the sounds of
'real news' to the
voices of the earth
Speaking
Saying what we would rather
not
Signing our names in
visible ink
Teaching when we can, understanding
when we can't
Singing love songs
LOUD
Creating
Beauty and sharing it
Creating
new ways to live where
what we build doesn't
destroy
A safe shared space with such joy
others emulate
Crying
for the children
at a war as unnecessary as
all wars
for all that is lost to us when we don't
see that
Seeing
is where vision is inside
seeing where we
and the one are
One
Remembering
where we come from
that we are no different
and there is no separation
Remembering our mistakes so
we can be

Forgiving
of ourselves
of others always
Lending
a hand
and whatever else
we can
Loving
for the sheer joy
of it, for the blessings it bestows
Laughing
with our inner voice
with the earth
Living
a life lived simply
Gentle steps
Small bites
Deep breaths
Ferreting out our fears
Frequent prayers
and Giving back better
and always
Hoping and
Knowing
that
violence will disappear as soon as we
conquer our fears
Knowing that
The Earth provides all we
really need
and she will
heal, even if we don't
Knowing that
Justice always wins
we just don't always see it

Sioban Lanigan

May We Be Blessed

May we be blessed by
the spirits of these fish
swimming through our world
from the world above
from the world below
rising from the depths of our future
blessing the depths of our past

Gary Lawless

Easter Morning, 2004

The first song, a noisy wren over the wet grass.
The next a repeated buzz in a bush, like a rattler snapping her tail.
The third an uproar of finches, the forth low murmurs of quail.
It is time to decide what the day has already decided,
to greet with song the rattler, the fox, the cat, the gun.
Listen. Somewhere in that sound is forgiveness.
So many songs. Bees humming in the purple ears of sage.
A motorcycle cackling happily up the canyon road.
Television announcing a ceasefire in mad Fallujah.
And underneath it all, the low unbowing of bent grass.
Are you listening?
Are you ready to step into the deep ocean of morning?
Are you listening?

Jim Lenfestey

The Song of the Ground

I clothed him in
buckskin, soft against hard
sinew. He held tight

to his bones. The cords
in his neck strained
against the silence

then softened
as the deer
came over him.

Softened
like the deer pulled
by prayer to the arrow,

he leaned into my hands
smoothing his hair to
his shoulders, baring

his pulse where the quiver
of snared sparrows
told me he expected

a rung throat, scalded
feathers, a meal
of sucked bones.

But when I began
to braid feathers in his
unbound hair

with my fingers soft
as down-tipped arrows—
he let go.

A roar of ferns
unfurled in green waves

across the forest floor

as I drew my bow,
reaching back to the moment
the word was born

from the air's desire
to be touched
by blood and bone,

passing through
precise as an arrow
who drops us to our knees

in the ferns where
I give myself like
rain on the ocean

aware I will break,
the future made whole
by our loving

the moment
I release the arrow
feather-tipped, my fingers

gathering his heart
still beating
to bury

in the song of the ground.

Jen Lighty

Deep Gap Haiku

Fog on the Blue Ridge
blinds me from the Deep Gap turn.
Lost, I feel at home.

Glenna Luschei

Henry Braun

We are given weight
  separate from the earth
  as the first miracle.
  —Henry Braun

He says a poem
  as if he were eating a ripe
    and heavy peach that fell
willingly into his hand
  in August in Georgia
    or Tennessee under
a peach tree where
  leaves of sunlight
    dance around him, on him
like the play of light
  on a dolphin's back.
    He turns it carefully,
examining the fruit
  for the next best bite
    as heavy drops of juice
settle in his palm
  before they gladly fall
    to the ground,
and congeal with soft dirt
  into glistening,
    succulent words.

Norm Minnick

Anchorage

A tomboy climbing a dirt hill rubs the dirt into her blue jeans. There's one open window in the Ten Commandments Club. Tenement faces which they called civilization on the violent crushing slopes of frontier. Mountains crash into swollen eyes, with sun-jagged rocks in July snow barely melting. If you found yourself here, alone and hungry. Maybe you'd learn to pray.
Sun is rising.
Seagull took pine into ocean to learn its lean voice. The hoarse squall of waves, a fragile balance as making a space to breathe   cup your hands and beg.
Where would pride?
Is it the vessel to strive through this pain?   But often it was the flat clouds.
Dee 247 1102 anytime.
Drawn inward, a tight cord
we seek quickly the confession.
Human nature stretched clean
every element recycled.
Simple for old tires to replace
dandelions
to blow wishes.

Trey Moore

Fall in Love with Your Life

Fall in love with your life
    too big of a statement
    to even attempt
How about
    fall in love with your house
    or
    fall in love with your mother
    or leave them
    Eckhart Tolle writes, "Accept a situation or leave it,
    all else is madness."
A world full of madness
    internal battles of right and wrong
    false and showy appearances
Fall in love with your life
    or the leaf on that table
    or the dog on your doorstep

Can you fall in love with the light at dawn
    or your husband's key
    in the door?
Maybe you can fall in love
    with that song on the radio
    and when you don't
    turn it off
Can you fall in love with silence
 and spaces
    and not knowing?
Can you accept them at least?
Or must you continue running
 from moments of idleness
    to your list of important
 things to do

Can you trust
    for one moment
    that you have
    all
    the time

you need?
Can you believe
     for one hour
     that there is a master plan
     that does not involve you
     scurrying and rushing
     through life?
Fall in love with your life
     or maybe
     just a conversation with a friend
     a poem
     a star in the night sky
Fall in love with the urges that motivate you
     and the flies that bite you
     and the disgust
     that pushes them away
Love all that pushes you away
Trust it to guide you
     in the right
     direction

Tammy Nelson

Crows

If only I could explain what the body knows,
that our blood is a drop of open ocean,
that the creatures living inside us have lived
for millions of years as the bottom feeders of history.
So much there is no explanation for, like
how a machete can be thought to solve a dispute,
or how crumbs of stale bread will secure for the wanderer
a direct way home. Some days the membrane lining
my gut is on fire. My mind twists like intestines
attempting to figure things out,
like why we have a word for peace but only talk of war.
Or why the mistakes we have already proven
are the same mistakes we enact all over again.
I don't know about you, but the black crows
sitting on the telephone wire in today's grey fog
seem ominous to me. Their cries and caws are not songs,
their big bodies burden the taught wire. Of course
I am supposed to disregard such signs from nature,
driving past on my way to one obligation or another.
Of course it seems of little consequence just how many crows sit
staring into the horizonless distance. But something tells me
they know what I want to know. Something in their bodies
can explain what my body lacks a vocabulary for. You see
how unafraid they are? You see how still they sit in this cold fog?

Margaret Paul

Poem for Frederick

Driving back from a night at the shore
between hills green with new rye grass. Home,
I see in my neighbor's yard the year's first
iris bud. The purple of that almost-here
flower, makes me remember that Frederick
wanted a winter poem by tonight for The Crow.
Well, here it is, a day late, finished up
in a coffee shop, Super Bowl Sunday,
temperature in the fifties, air moist,
low gray clouds moving in a slow scud.
There's skiing three hours drive away
I won't go, yet I have "a mind of winter."
Well again. It isn't finished. I type
a week later. Now jonquils and daffodils,
and when I walk my dog, I see heron like
white clouds nesting in a still barren tree.
Yet my winter mind dozes in its burrow
refusing to come out of long sleep.
Three or four years later, still not finished,
and you now sleep the longest sleep. Frederick,
this year I missed the gravity of your smile in the dining hall
where we once leaned on coffee and waited for sunrise.
So fierce you were against injustice, at such a cost.
You would not dance, but there was such a longing in you.

Nils Peterson

Table Top

Long and straight, a smooth and useful surface,
Good for cooking or eating or paying your debts,
To keep all the vipers at bay, to keep
A sturdy lid on the shadow world below;
Meanwhile, a lively game of five-card stud
Is dealt out every day at sunup.
When winter sets in, its cracks widen.
A man could get waylaid in those gullies.
You have to stay awake, ready to slip through,
Ready to spiral and darken like a pine knot,
To be marked with the names of failed loves,
Slowly turning, turning.
On your right shoulder, a shade with a whisper
Like old varnish, is trying to call your bluff:
"You go on escaping through those openings,
You'll be homeless. Oh, yes, you praise the laws
Of chance, but you pay the light bill right on time,
You keep the weeds down, you even pray."
Pay no heed. Without apology or regret,
The lucky man knows this run can't last,
The wrong card will turn up, or maybe
It's the only one left on the table,
Then darkness will come as another gift,
At first a bitter taste, then cool water.

Michael Quam

It Has Come To This

I can't go anywhere
without you now. Like
the farmer in springtime
I carry you with me
like seed scattering you
through whatever field I wander.
It seems that everything has
been plowed, everything is ready
to receive you. And yet
there's this loneliness. As if
any letting go of you
diminishes me, as if I
may not be the harvester;
and a greed sets in, the single
note tolling "more," "more,"
calling me to prayer so that
each new growth in me
or you will age into a wine
that might appease the gods
of distance until they
fall asleep side by side
and dream us together again.

Fran Quinn

On the Sandhill Crane Migration Route in November

Five silos always line Hwy. 29.
At least in my small always.
Five silos were not
always. Hwy. 29 was not
always, but always
the ways of cranes sang
in bones hollowed for flight,
in blood tuned towards the narrow
halls of north.
What is my always?
Is it resurrection
how the bare branches fill
with the smell of burnt leaves?

Katie Rauk

Stuttering Boy

stuttering boy
stammers out the words
that are afraid to come out
never gets to say what's in his heart:

"l-l-love"
he never gets to say "I l-l-love you"
to the b-b-beautiful girl

the teenager stammers
looking for new words
to create a new reality
for his g-g-generation
trying to speak his own vision
for his own time
in b-b-broken words
a b-b-breakaway from the past

in the Bible
Moses stuttered when he saw the bush
rise into flame
and said:
"my g-g-god
hu-hu-who are you?
and again before Pharoah
as he saw his rod turn into serpent:
"Let my p-p-people g-g-go"
with this stutter
astonished
he turned slavery into freedom

the poet continuously stutters
never knowing what words
are going to c-c-come next
from mouth or p-p-pen

the miraculous stutter
transforming

vision into sound
feeling into words
voice into l-l-language

Joe Shakarchi

Reflection, This Fall

The river takes donations from the trees:
loosened leaves
make a liquid russet hem. The sun joins in.
What's up, what's down?
My heart goes to the Kennedys: John John,
his wife, her sister flying
towards the sea. They couldn't tell the sky
from water.

When Hamlet tells his friend Horatio
who's come to see a father's funeral
"I think it was to see my mother's
wedding" we know the world
is out of joint. And that's the thrust: rot and
beauty oozing, blurring boundaries
to dust. "Down the hatch" becomes
a toast or eulogy. In October

my mind's a riddled door. I have to laugh-*a bodkin,*
another century's word, arrives to
needle holes inside my head.
        My husband
walks into the room (when I am writing)
with his pain: the morning's headline's
Violence in Jerusalem
lines he wants to mend, while I continue to
pretend sun rises, poems save, sun sets.

Myra Shapiro

Reporting From a Night on Lake Damariscotta

I lie awake listening to waves lick the shore,
the drone of a motor boat in the distance
silenced by the cry of a loon.
Someone plays a guitar in a cabin nearby.
Sleepless, I leave the tent,
walk down to the water
carefully stepping between lady-slipper and ivy,
slipping on loose stones.
The smell of a distant bonfire reaches me-
burned birch and maple.
Intoxicating, I breathe in the smoke.

The pier rocks, beating against its liquid pedestal
while above, a shooting star falls and
another follows in pursuit.
Across the lake the lonely loon cries again;
This time its mate answers from the other side.
Taking up the call, bachelor bullfrogs croak in unison-
all on the make. The one slightly off key and a trifle slow
will not make the hump.
Minnows dart beneath the shadows looking for
someone special?
My eyes scraping the waterscape
spot a lone canoe passing the island of pine and fir.
Behind me a soft snore breaks my reverie.
I return, content, to fill our sleeping bag.

Carol Sheldon

Lake Stone

(After Charles Simic)

You know the kind -those oval, fine-grained ones
you can find on the shore of any lake.
Buffeted and polished by waves is best,
sleek from having rubbed shoulders with fish,
spun and turned and danced under the surface
so as to achieve their smooth complexion.
Go into a stone like that.
Stand in a room lined with reed mats,
softly wet underfoot, the air smelling green
though not brackish. Down a narrow hallway
there's a fireplace. Someone who has lived here
since the ocean receded owns this place.
He squats atop a throne of snail shells
draped with feathery water-weeds.
His round, flat eyes blink in the half-dark,
cold thighs elongate to webbed feet.
Hear the sound of his flute, an empty crab-leg,
as you step forward to ask to marry his daughter.

Thomas R. Smith

At Palisades Nuclear Power Plant

Waves lap the sand the sand the sand
and while we keep silence, the silence of Annabelle Lee
a plutonium fuel rod ticks away
stored on the dunes where we used to play.
We played Elephants on a Spider Web
Sword of Damocles
Go Fish.

Peaceful atoms take millenia
to decay.

Barbara Spring

August Ending

Twisting the nozzle I thin the fan
of hose water, tilting it
so that it flows over
dusty flowers. Where spray touches
evening a hummingbird
stands still in air to gather
thousands of water drops
in his thousands of wingbeats.

Frank Steele

Pebbles

A run of pebbles at the drip line
under the eaves, at the edge
of the grass, mostly brown
except when picked out by water.
Then they gleam, treasures
you forgot you ever had—
reds, orange, blues, yellow, opal
the high highlights of a soft rain
up from the Gulf, the glory
of what's in reserve.
You can't be a collector.
In your pocket they go flat.
But where rain pulls its curtain
around your porch, the pebbles
will bloom and show the edge
of home and someplace else,
and even take you there.

Peggy Steele

In the Company of Great People

I plant a tiny grain of longing,
And when the sun, soil and rain have had their way,
I gather the ripened amber wheat,strip it on the threshing floor,
and store it away.

When the mouse comes under cover of darkness,
It takes my longing through the tall grass,
to sleep inside the walls of someone else's home.

And when they drive it out, surely the falcon will find it.
When the talons and beak sink in,
the mouse struggles, it quivers,
as it must when flesh is torn from bone.

But how long will it take to become the falcon,
soaring over mountain, over sea,
and rising to the sun?

Echo Trobridge

Seven Haiku for Summer 2008

1.
moon over Kieve
loons on the once only lake
this time for Richie
2.
poppies line the way
we are bringing songs to try
everyone listens
3.
Great Mother Conference
sweetness blooming for breakfast
petals in the wind
4.
frog song. telling jokes.
something serious about
to happen. or not.
5.
Frank Steele   Henry Braun
and Naomi Shihab Nye
Franny Quinn's in tears
6.
Robert and Coleman
laughter filling Innisfree
tabla and sitar
7.
morning on the porch
people quietly finding words
without speaking them

Jim Watt

Gratitude In Telluride

In a room in the old train depot
We set books on the table.
Only one man & a facilitator
Come to our workshop.
The man lives at ten thousand feet
In an old mining cabin.
Paints houses all summer in Aspen.
Drives cab in the winter &
Snow mobiles home. He asks a smart
Question. In what way does the
Work of the three Reed College friends
Inform our own. His question
Helps us frame what we're doing.
In a way it all comes down to
Gratitude. Snyder, Whalen, & Welch
Taught us craft, manhood, lore
Of the tribe, as Williams taught
Them. They gave us permission
To enter the stream running
From old Walt & to add our
Tributaries to that great American
      River of song.

Phil Woods